The *Soul* of SUCCESS

ESSENTIALS THAT POSITION YOU TO PROSPER FOR LIFE

DARRYL READE

To order the printed version and for all other inquiries please write to:

strategicsolutionsgroup@yahoo.com

ACKNOWLEDGMENTS

This book is dedicated to my father, Jack, whose integrity and wisdom left an indelible mark on my life, and to my wife, Cynthia, for her insightfulness and support.

I also want to thank my supporters, believers, and doubters for each one in their own way made me a stronger and more adaptable person as well as making my life richer.

Cover Design by Emily Foreit

CONTENTS

CONTENTS

CONTENTS

BACKGROUND

I was a curious soul. I asked questions. I listened more than I talked. I learned that you didn't have to be the loudest voice in the room to make a difference. I tried to learn something new each and every day and to apply that knowledge in useful and meaningful ways.

I understood there is not one way you had to do things to be successful. Whereas many people are rigid slaves to their routines I had no qualms about trying something different.

I was dedicated to driving excellence for myself as well as accelerating, fueling, and steering others to achieve similar positive results.

I always thought of myself as a transformational leader, a change agent, a visionary, and one who had the strength of character and courage of conviction to fight for what was right.

I was drawn to the publishing business, excelled at what I did, and was recognized for my efforts by being named Advertising Age's Best and Brightest.

At each level I gained insight into building and empowering teams, influencing business processes, and for championing corporate initiatives that both delivered and maximized profitability.

Success depends on consistently winning the hearts and minds of people both in business and in life. This book shows you how by identifying core principles and values necessary to achieve and sustain it.

FOREWORD

I always had a desire to help others and to give back in some way and this book provides such a platform.

The Soul of Success puts a fresh face on what separates success from failure and gives you the optimal chance, not just to achieve what you want but to feel good about it too. It provides insights that lead to better outcomes and better decision-making; strategies for bolstering all aspects of the sales cycle as well as the essentials required to open doors, create opportunities, validate your value, and cultivate respect.

It also is intended to reinforce the notion that we all have within us the ability to transform our circumstances and turn our passion into reality. This book will challenge you to tap your inner Picasso and to dream to do extraordinary things.

Success is not predetermined at birth. It does not happen by chance. It begins with aspiration but the payoff comes with perspiration.

CHAPTER I

BUILDING A FOUNDATION
FOR SUSTAINED SUCCESS

THE FUNDAMENTALS

Here are tried-and-true approaches that you will come to treasure for both their simplicity and effectiveness. They are based on life lessons and best practices which, when integrated into a daily routine, will enable one to produce exceptional results.

Relationships
Don't ever underestimate the value of the personal relationship. The right chemistry can be the deciding factor in winning or retaining business.

Under-Promise and Over-Deliver
Customers appreciate diligence and extra effort and will reward you for it.

You will never hear a client saying they are disappointed when you exceed their expectations. When you over- deliver you have a happier customer and one more inclined to let you capture a greater share of their wallet.

Right Stuff
You'll grow big by thinking small. Pay attention to details, the little things. It is tough to be 100% better than your competitors - but you can be 1% better in a hundred different ways.

Moment of Truth

Anyone who has ever done cold calling or prospecting by telephone knows there is a 10-15 second window of opportunity to get your message across and pique interest. Failure to do so may lose whatever chance you had to make the initial sale and to garner repeat business.

Listening

Wisdom is what you get for a lifetime of listening. Do not underestimate the importance of listening. The successful salesperson is cognizant of the fact that you can sometimes be more effective by saying less.

Be Resolute

Do not expect to take away business from a competitor based on a single interaction. People absorb portions of your message in pieces. Maintain visibility. Continue to tout your core competencies. Each contact puts you one step closer to capturing new business and retaining it in subsequent years.

Know When To Let Go

Your time is valuable. It is also finite. Fight for the business, but be perceptive enough to know when to move on. You'll find some accounts are not financially worth your time and effort.

The sooner you are able to recognize when these situations occur and when to let go, the more successful you will be.

The Thrill of Victory and the Agony of Defeat
If this doesn't describe your feelings maybe selling is not your cup of tea.

Handling Objections
In the martial arts we practice katas or forms until the moves become second nature. Apply the same approach to handling objections. Compile a list. Think of different responses. Fine tune. Refine. Keep practicing. You will begin to see positive results.

Passionate about What You Are Doing
It has been said that enthusiasm is contagious. People are more likely to buy from people who are passionate about what they are selling.

Doing a Few Things Exceptionally Well
Vince Lombardi, the Hall of Fame football coach, relied on just a few offensive plays to score points. Lombardi liked to keep his system simple. He believed it was not how many different plays they had in the playbook - but how well they executed those they used. Know your strengths and capitalize on those to win business.

Types of Buyers

I am not a great proponent of categorizing buyers into groups with fancy and sometimes hard to pronounce monikers. I like to think of them as either conventional or uncon-ventional. The former will try to maintain the status quo at all costs and the latter will be more willing to take calculated risks. Spend time with both, but the road to success will be quicker and far easier with the unconventional buyer because he or she sees change as an opportunity to enhance his or her business.

Keep It Simple

"Brevity is the best recommendation of speech whether in a senator or an orator" (Cicero). It is better to make a few memorable points rather than none at all.

Targeting

Reach out to all the people who can affect the buying decision. Not only the decision makers but those I refer to as influencers, persuaders, and shapers. Create dialogues with these different constituencies. They have the ability to deliver your message in ways that can enhance your credibility and relevancy with buyers. This leads to success by eliminating whatever barriers there may be to making the sale.

Unique Selling Proposition
Clearly communicate your company's core competencies. Illustrate that you can do some things that the competition cannot. For example, do you have a technological edge? Do you run 24/7 for time- sensitive clients? Do you have any mechanisms in place, such as a special event, which can showcase a customer's products? Do you have access to market intelligence that can help clients uncover emerging trends?
By continuing to look for creative ways to differentiate and distance oneself from the competition will position you to win and retain more business as well as heighten your chances for long-term success.

Attrition
Minimize its impact by casting the widest possible net. Keep adding to your prospect list; broaden your client base; and nurture existing accounts in order to build incremental business.

Thank You
Always make time to thank customers for their business. Why? "Kind words can be short and easy to speak, but their echoes are truly endless" (Mother Theresa).

Preparation

Louis Nizer, the world-renowned trial lawyer was asked by TV host Johnny Carson what led to his success in the courtroom. "Many lawyers were more talented and eloquent than myself," he said. "What gave me the edge was preparation."

Always remember results are linked to execution and execution starts with the fundamentals.

A MAN OF FEW WORDS

Abraham Lincoln made what many believe is the greatest speech in U.S. history. Known as the Gettysburg Address, it was just 269 words and took up just two minutes of his audience's time. His predecessor on the platform was famed orator Edward Everett who talked more than two hours but do folks remember anything noteworthy he said that day?

Think of those you place in high regard or those you have the utmost respect. Do they talk more or talk less?

PYRRHIC VICTORY
KNOW WHEN TO LET GO

Think about winning the war not just the battle. Know when to walk away from a situation. Cut your losses. Don't try to secure new or incremental business if you are expected to continually accept unreasonable terms.

In the book *Art Of War,* Sun Tzu sees the role of a general, in part, to consist of creating changes and manipulating them to his advantage. The excellent general weighs the situation before he moves. He does not blunder aimlessly into baited traps. He is prudent, but not hesitant. He realizes that there are some roads not to be followed, some not to be attacked, some cities not to be besieged, and some positions not to be contested. He takes calculated risks but not needless ones.

Under certain conditions one yields a city, sacrifices a portion of a force, or gives ground in order to gain a more valuable objective. Such yielding therefore masks a deeper purpose and is but another aspect of the intellectual pliancy that distinguishes the expert in war.

Sometimes you gain more by saying no. Remember this point: no one is in business to lose money. Let the competition score their pyrrhic victories. However, it will be you who is the last one standing.

FISH WISELY AND FISH
WHERE THE FISH ARE

I have always believed that the truly successful salesperson not only works harder but also works smarter. Did you ever take the time to evaluate your customer list? To identify and differentiate customers based on long-term value and profitability? To determine the frequency of purchase and the size of each sale?

Do the exercise, and you might be surprised to find out that you are spending too much time with accounts that may only help you maintain the status quo rather than exceed corporate revenue goals for your territory or region.

Always remember to fish wisely and to fish where the fish are, for it is not the size of your customer list but the quality of the list that counts.

SITTING ON A GOLDMINE?
<u>COULD BE A LANDMINE</u>

Have you spent lots of time trying to woo that dream account? The one you think will make your career or help to put you on easy street? Have you done all of the right things to garner a bigger piece of the revenue pie from an existing account - only to maintain the status quo?

Have you ever read about the advertising agency creative shootouts that can cost each agency hundreds of thousands of dollars at their own expense - with nothing in the end to show for it?

Have you thought about which accounts are winnable or when the cost to pursue new business becomes too high?

A sales manager I know was very proud of a story he chose to share with me about how he made repeated calls to the decision maker of one company and through his determination finally got the opportunity to bid on an upcoming project. He faxed a written proposal to the buyer and later was told that his numbers looked good. A few days passed before the buyer called back and said, that the incumbent underbid my friend's proposal by 30%.

Given the opportunity to counter- offer, my friend's reply at the time was not what the buyer expected. He stated that his company did consistently good work at reasonable prices.

He felt his offer was aggressive and that he could not go any lower. He told the buyer to give him a call back when the incumbent was no longer in business. A year later he did get that phone call and has been the preferred vendor ever since.

Sometimes you need to draw a line in the sand. Sometimes you have to say no to get a yes. Remember to do your due diligence. Assess and reassess the benefit of utilizing both your time and the company's resources in order to make the sale.

Persistence is a good thing, but do not let persistence and determination get in the way of seeing the signals that indicate when it's the right time to move on. Remember: if it appears to be too good to be true, it probably is.

Are you sitting on a goldmine, or could it be a landmine?

NARRATIVES: SHOULD I GO LEFT OR RIGHT?

I went to the liquor store to get an expert opinion
about several wines I had heard about. I approached one of the wine consultants and asked for his opinion. Here is what he said:

Bottle #1
Even the smell is mind-blowing. It is massive, ripe and chewy, with a remarkable combination of big fruit and tight structure.

Bottle #2
This one is vibrant and alive, with bright tastes of raspberries and dark chocolate. Elegant and restrained, but with just enough bite to give it an extra dimension.

Bottle #3
Effortlessly classy, with structured cherry-berry fruit and excellent acids that make it great with food.

Consumers are known to have a penchant to act more often when messaging is based on emotion rather than on the data. That is why embellishing or shading the truth is such an effective marketing tool.

Spin usually works best when you have similar products or services. When properly defined it helps to build awareness, interest, and desire. All critical elements along the path to purchase.

While your efforts should be on selling the tangible benefits of a product or service do not underestimate the intangibles and just how meaningful a part they can play in gaining a competitive edge.

Without the right narrative something terrible happens. Nothing! Sometimes the choice is not should I go left or right but how best to get from point A to point B.

DO YOU HAVE A KITCHEN CABINET?

After Hurricane Katrina hit, no one appeared to have entered President Bush's office to say, "This is really bad." And apparently he first learned of the severity of the Abu Ghraib prison scandal from the media. Could a "Kitchen Cabinet" - a group of trusted advisers not in government - have changed how Bush handled these as well as other critical issues?

Because presidents and their staffs live an isolated existence, good outside advice is important. Just like presidents, we all need sounding boards, reliable sources who we can count on that will pull no punches and tell us how things really are.

If you want to make good decisions seek out people of different backgrounds and beliefs; brainstorm for new ideas and perspectives; become proficient in developing alternative points of view. Always remind yourself that for a Kitchen Cabinet to be useful, one must be open to disagreements.

Not surprisingly, those presidents who regularly sought contradictory opinions were considered to be among our best - including Lincoln, FDR, Truman, and Reagan.

Do you have a Kitchen Cabinet? If not, maybe it is time for you to start thinking about the advantages of having one.

NURTURING INTELLIGENCE
FOR ANY SURFACE

Roger Federer is one of those athletes who come along only once a decade or generation. His impact on the game of tennis can't be measured by titles alone. What may be his most important legacy is not his movements on the court or his classy carriage off it but his intelligent approach to the game.

If players want to compete, they must adapt to both their opponents and the playing surfaces. It is important to learn and adjust and to decode the subtleties of grass, clay, and concrete. To thrive, one must avoid a one-dimensional and mechanical approach. One must be resourceful as well as robotic. Intelligence isn't manufactured but nurtured. Federer uses his skills, technique, tactics, and mind to win matches.

Welcome to the Federer Era where nurturing intelligence for any surface is a battle-tested approach that will put you on the right course to succeed.

FALLING PREY TO COMPLACENCY

Being satisfied and comfortable with something is a good feeling. But it can be costly. Leading companies in various industries routinely question every operation and every policy in an effort to better manage their resources and maximize profitability.

Just like the leading companies, successful salespeople recognize that they cannot fall prey to complacency. Start looking for sacred cows of your own – the convenient old practices or fixed ideas which might be adversely affecting your sales efforts.

Have you tried any new ways or approaches to tell your story? Do you take a consultative approach or push the value proposition? Are you a good listener? A problem-solver? Are you looking for ways to establish long-term relationships? Have you seriously thought about the best time to do prospecting? Have you stopped using corporate-supplied collateral materials? Have you stopped calling on prospects after the first NO?

I would encourage every one to periodically do a self-evaluation. Make a list of your own sacred cows. You may find one or two that may be keeping you from reaching your full potential. The wise salesperson will look to cast aside practices and ideas that may no longer be timely or beneficial.

WORKING THE EROGENOUS ZONES

Working the erogenous zones - a.k.a. developing rapport - is a subject that is often overlooked, yet it is critical to success. It helps you to establish trust and earn a prospect's confidence. It prevents others from acting defensively in your presence and makes it less likely you will come across as demanding, arrogant, and overzealous.

Compliment the successes and achievements of others. Listen attentively. Don't let yourself be distracted while someone is speaking to you. Make eye contact - and a concerted effort to give others time to finish their thoughts before adding your own views. Interrupting before the completion of others' sentences devalues them and what they have to say and can also spark feelings of animosity. Learn to take a personal interest in your prospects. Find out what they are passionate about. Spend quality time with them.

You need to work the erogenous zones in order to sell someone something or to ask that they do something on your behalf. It is the key to creating nourishing and meaningful relationships. It enables one to become far more effective when dealing with others and encourages people to want to do business with you.

GROUNDED IN LIFE SKILLS

If you think getting to the top is all about achievement, you are wrong. But what exactly does it take to reach this lofty goal?

One perspective is that promotion decisions can be very subjective, dependent on perception as well as output. Companies look for people who are good working in teams, people who show the potential to grow the business organically through enhancing the reputation of the firm and by developing loyal client relationships. Luck, too, plays a role - as well as the all-important relationships formed between junior and more senior executives.

While performance is critical to success, it is not always enough. Grounding oneself in mainstream
cultural and life skills is also necessary if you want to keep moving up the ladder and eventually make it to the top.

CHAPTER II

MASTERING THE HABITS OF SUCCESSFUL PEOPLE

BEST OF THE BEST

W. Clement Stone was not an imposing figure. He dyed the hair on his head and his pencil thin mustache jet black. Some people may have perceived him as being odd. He was also very rich and very successful. He ran an insurance empire now known as AON Corporation. Mr. Stone was the personification of the quintessential salesperson. He is famous for having a positive mental attitude. His mantra was "I feel healthy. I feel happy. I feel terrific!" Stone's idea about the ability of a determined and optimistic person to rise above any obstacle is as timely today as when he began his business career. His life and legacy are evidence of that.

Steve Fossett was living proof of the old adage: If at first you don't succeed, try, try again. Fossett tried six times before he became the first person to fly a balloon solo around the world. He was known for setting his sights on a goal and then relentlessly pursuing it. He learned from each failure and put those lessons to work in subsequent attempts.

Nolan Ryan, a Hall of Fame baseball player, owes his success not so much to natural ability and talent as to hard work. Nolan always led by example. He was a workout-aholic. That is how he lasted so long. Twenty years after coming to the big leagues, teammates still marveled at his work ethic. At the start of every season he was prepared for the challenges that lie ahead.

The best of the best are a diverse group, but for all their differences they share common traits that transcend specific skill sets.

These individuals:

Possess more detailed and thorough knowledge of their competition, the customer's organization, and the market dynamics of that industry.

Convey determination, enthusiasm, optimism; ask the right questions, and are good listeners.

Are better prepared, more proactive, and skilled in relationship building.

Sell strategic solutions, not just products and have an unfailing dedication to their customers' success as well as their own.

The best of the best truly love what they do and work extremely hard at mastering their craft. Success comes at a price. You have to be willing pay for it.

DIFFERENCES IN STYLE
BUT THE SAME OUTCOME

There were two college basketball coaches. One was characterized by high fashion and the well-known creations of Armani and Ferragamo, the other by the more traditional creations of Levi and Lands' End.

The first coach espoused a wide-open offense and the run-and-shoot type of game while the second focused on a get-in-your-face defense.

Although one was an Armani and the other a Levi type guy, they were alike. Each set the bar high and stressed discipline, staying focused, and not taking anything for granted.

Examine successful sales people. The qualities that define them are:

- They seek answers and master skills.
- They are never complacent.
- They are passionate about what they do.
- They are good listeners.
- They are good communicators.
- They exceed clients' expectations for service.
- They are single-minded of purpose.
- They ask questions and solve problems.

1 PERCENT INSPIRATION AND 99 PERCENT PERSPIRATION

As human beings we want to believe that creativity and innovation come in flashes of pure brilliance, with great thunderclaps and echoing ahas. Innovators and other creative types, we believe, stand apart from the crowd, wielding secrets and magical talents beyond the rest of us.

Balderdash. Instead, innovation is a slow process of accretion, building small insight upon interesting fact upon tried-and-true process. The aha moments grow out of hours of thought and study.

Success does not happen by chance. It begins with inspiration but the payoff comes with perspiration.

JUST KEEP DOING IT

Exercise physiologists acknowledge that numerous repetitions over a long period of time are required for a muscle to perform a specific movement. Then, and only then, will you be able to properly perform the technique without thinking about it.

Masters of any activity - athletes and musicians alike - share one thing in common: they practice significantly more than people who are merely good or competent at what they do. The virtuoso pianist practices the scale 10,000 times just as the martial arts master practices a kick 10,000 times.

Remember mastering any event in life requires you to Just keep doing it.

THE STORY OF THE DARUMA DOLL

There is a saying associated with the Daruma Doll – "to fall seven times, to rise eight times, life starts from now."

The Daruma Doll is named after an ancient Chinese Zen Master, Bodidharma, and is symbolic of his self-discipline and positive outlook.

Its weighted bottom and rounded shape forces this ancient cultural doll to right itself after being knocked over, and through this process we are taught how dedication, resilience, and persistence can help convert life's setbacks into future successes.

The Daruma doll comes with both eyes blank. Upon purchasing or receiving it as a gift, you paint one eye and make a wish when you begin a new project.

The second eye is painted when the wish comes true or the project is completed.

The Daruma doll is a constant reminder of the important role persistence and determination play in achieving one's goals.

POKER IS NOT ONLY ABOUT THE CARDS

What lessons can be learned from this great American pastime? Poker is not about winning and losing as much as what it can teach us about how to achieve success in whatever endeavor we may choose in life.

Poker aficionados have learned to hone one's vocational skills, like assessing risk, reading the faces of rivals, leveraging strengths, masking weaknesses, and coping with stress.

The best poker players can identify opponents' "tells" - patterns of behavior, such as gestures or movements, that give away their hands. This skill gives them a big advantage in their business dealings, especially in negotiations. Others have said poker has taught them the value of human contact, the personal interaction that helps in solidifying relationships.

There are lessons to be learned from this game. Continue to reflect on these skill sets, and don't be surprised to see similarities among those that consistently win at the poker table, succeed in the boardroom, or are great at closing the deal.

DARE TO THINK <u>DIFFERENTLY</u>

The odds were stacked against two Australian scientists trying to prove that a bacterial infection - not stress or spicy food - caused attacks of gastritis and peptic stomach ulcers.

The scientific community, the medical establishment, and drug companies refused for years to accept such a radical theory. It would upset established science: the accepted treatment was surgery, psychological counseling, and drugs that blocked production of gastric acid.

But Dr. Barry Marshall and Dr. Robin Warren persevered. They proved that an infection of the Helicobacter Pylori bacterium was the source for nearly all stomach ulcers. That meant such ulcer could be treated with antibiotics rather than surgery, easing recovery from this chronic, frequently disabling condition for thousands of sufferers.

There are instructive lessons here. Conventional wisdom is, well, conventional. It's the accepted and customary way we've done things, and sometimes it's dead wrong. When faced with such daunting opposition, it is necessary to persevere – to prove that a radical theory can become the new convention.

As is often the case when a new theory surfaces, the opposition has a vested interest in the status quo. Surgeons had been assured of a steady stream of ulcer patients, as were counselors who promoted lifestyle changes as an answer to ulcers. Drug companies also profited: H2 blockers eased symptoms and made ulcers disappear. But they didn't cure what turned out to be the underlying bacterial infection, so there were plenty of relapses and the drugs had to be taken repeatedly.

Dr. Marshall became so convinced the bacterium was the culprit and antibiotics the cure that he swallowed some of the bacteria, got sick, and treated himself successfully with antibiotics. Both he and his colleague, Dr. Warren, were honored for their discovery by being presented with the 2005 Nobel Prize in medicine.

Successful people get the coveted prize because they dare to think differently, challenge prevailing dogmas, and display the power of perseverance. They do not walk away when adversity strikes. They meet challenges head-on and stay the course.

IF YOUR FRIENDS JUMPED OFF A BRIDGE, WOULD YOU?

Sure, it's always easier to go with the crowd than to voice disagreement. As a professed contrarian (or voice of reason as I prefer to spin), if you say white, there is a good chance I will say black. It's not because I want to challenge your choice of colors for the sake of challenging. Rather, I will start wondering why black might not be a better choice.

Often those who aspire to be contrarian are the ones who make giant scores - because they see opportunity where others don't.

Challenge the herd. Step out from the comfort zone of popular opinion or what is considered conventional wisdom. Take calculated risks.

DARK IN HERE - KNOW WHEN
YOU'VE GOT A GOOD THING

A woman takes a lover during the day while her husband is at work. Her nine-year-old son comes home unexpectedly, so she puts the son in the closet and shuts the door. Her husband comes home minutes later, so she puts her lover in the closet with the little boy. The little boy says, "Dark in here."

The man says:	Yes it is.
Boy:	I have a baseball.
Man:	That's nice.
Boy:	Want to buy it?
Man:	No, thanks.
Boy:	My dad's outside.
Man:	OK, how much?
Boy:	$250.

In the next few weeks, it happens again that the boy and the lover are in the closet together.

Boy:	Dark in here.
Man:	Yes it is.
Boy:	I have a baseball glove.

The lover, remembering the last time, asks the boy, "How much?"

Boy:	$750.
Man:	Fine.

A few days later, the father says to the boy, "Grab your glove. Let's go outside and toss the baseball back and forth." The boy says, "I can't, I sold them." The father asks, "How much did you sell them for?"

Boy: $1000.

The father says, "That's terrible to overcharge your friends like that! That is way more than those two things cost.

I'm going to take you to church and make you confess." They go to the church and the dad makes the little boy sit in the confession booth. He closes the door.

The boy says, "Dark in here." The priest says, "Don't start that again!"

While it is said that in every successful negotiation everybody wins, more often than not, one party wins more than the other.

The key to getting what you want lies in knowing how to negotiate more effectively. It matters not whether the exchange is between buyers and sellers, family and friends, coaches and athletes. The principles are the same.

Remember, how you negotiate and interact with people is how every relationship or business transaction succeeds or falters.

CHAPTER III

CODE OF CONDUCT

DO WHAT'S RIGHT OR DON'T DO IT AT ALL

One can fall prey to unethical behavior or poor judgment when confronted with the potential loss of one's position and company perks as well as when put under unbearable pressure to meet ambitious goals. Goals made more difficult to reach due to not having the resources to get the job done right.

Arthur Andersen was once the most respected and largest of the big five public accounting firms, but they became so obsessed with revenue that the firm's leaders waffled on ethics – their company's and those of their clients. The once venerable firm strayed disastrously from its cherished maxim of "Think straight. Talk straight." This led unfortunately to their demise.

Barbara Toffler, in her book *Final Accounting*, says that Andersen was a place where the pursuit of revenues was Job #1. Partners told her to drive up billings, even if they were unjustified. And so exalted were the partners in Andersen's hierarchy-is-almighty milieu that underlings were afraid to speak up. Worse, thanks to a bizarre revenue crediting arrangement, staffers spent as much time trying to cut one another out of new business as they did trying to develop it. Andersen, she suggests, was a "brutally cutthroat" place where "I learned to try to screw someone else before they screwed me." Had Andersen stood by the ethics of its founder, it would be thriving today and setting the profession's highest standards - instead of being reviled for the lowest.

Remember to do it the right way - or don't do it at all. Resist the temptation to compromise your values. By being true to yourself you will be a winner in both business and your personal life.

IVY LEAGUE OR ALSO RAN?
DOES IT MATTER?

I was intrigued by a story written in the New York Times questioning whether an individual attending a highly selective and highly expensive college confers any real benefit in later life.

Two researchers, one being an economics professor from Princeton University, suggest there's no benefit. They found that students who chose a school with lower admissions standards over more competitive schools earned incomes just as high as those who attended elite colleges.

The research illustrates that a better predictor of your career success and future income have less to do with the college attended - and more to do with the character of the person.

TOUGH LOVE OR KID GLOVES?

Tony Dungy is a National Football League head coach with   achievements that make him among the most influential figures in the league.

Dungy has the highest winning percentage among active coaches, his signature defense has been widely copied, and he has played a large role in diversifying the current coaching fraternity. But the mark he is happiest about is a subtle shift in the conduct expected of successful coaches.

When Tony Dungy faced Lovie Smith at Super Bowl XLI, it was labeled the triumph of the nice guy. Implicit was the message that for a week, at least, the sport's biggest stage was devoid of the glower and bluster, the abject misery that defined the public image of so many coaches.

The N.F.L. is delighted to have Dungy as the new face of victory - not just because he is a minority success story, but because he is likable. Dungy's memoir, *"Quiet Strength,"* is a best seller, a testament not only to his coaching skills, but also to his broad appeal.

He has great patience, never panics, and has an unwavering belief in people he works with. He believes his calling was to teach football, but he would have failed if he did not also teach his players to be better men.

When Dungy was being considered for his first coaching job there was a concern he was too nice. Was he, in fact, going to be tough enough?

Tough love or kid gloves? Twenty six years later, the N.F.L. has its answer, and Dungy's career has made its imprint.

PACKING YOUR PARACHUTE

I recently received an email from a friend of mine that every manager and sales person should try to remember.

One day when Ben and his wife were sitting in a restaurant a man at another table came up and said, "You're Ben! You flew jet fighters in Korea. You were shot down."

"How in the world did you know that?" Ben asked. "I packed your parachute," the man replied. Ben gasped in surprise and gratitude. The other man said, "I guess it worked."

Ben assured him it did. "If your chute hadn't worked, I wouldn't be here today." That night, Ben wondered how many times he might have seen this airman and not even said good morning or anything else, because "I was a pilot and he was just an airman."

Ben thought of the many hours this airman had spent carefully weaving the shrouds and folding the silks of each chute, each time holding in his hands the fate of someone he didn't know.

We all have people who provide what we need to make it through each day. Sometimes in the daily challenges that life gives us, we miss what is really important. We may fail to say hello, please,

or thank you; congratulate someone on something wonderful that has happened to him; give a compliment; or just do something nice for no reason.

As you go through the coming days, weeks, months, and years, recognize people who pack your parachute. You will be rewarded for kindness and thoughtfulness.

CHAPTER IV

SAGE ADVICE

I CHING TEACHINGS

I CHING is one of the oldest and greatest works known to mankind. Long before writing came to China some 5000 years ago, its great wisdom was handed down from generation to generation in the oral tradition, perhaps for thousands of years.

According to I CHING teachings, constant change is the only thing that does not change. To remain inflexible when all else is changing is to invite disaster. It is essential to your success that you set a firm course and be stable enough in your character not to waver with every passing fad. Just as important is to be aware of changing conditions and flexible enough in your thinking to change with changing conditions.

Maintaining rigidity leads to failure; remaining flexible leads to success.

BE STRONG LIKE WATER

Bruce Lee, the renowned martial artist, once said: "Empty your mind. Be formless, shapeless, like water. If you put water into a cup, it becomes the cup. You put water into a bottle and it becomes the bottle. You put it in a teapot it becomes the teapot. Now, water can flow or it can crash. "Be water, my friend. "

Bruce Lee introduced a new martial arts system based in part on valuing the need to be adaptable and flexible. He had a great deal of success because instruction in other styles was often too rigid. Students were taught to commit moves to memory and to repeat them the same way every time. You can get by with this at the beginning levels, but by the time you reach the advanced levels you will find yourself at a serious disadvantage if your moves don't flex to deal with the dynamics of each individual situation. In the real world things don't always go down like they do in a textbook, and if you are the one who can create on the spur of the moment you are going to win.

It is important to be exposed to many different techniques, and then try to adapt them into your own game plan, but it is also important to recognize that some things will not work well for you.

Only you can decide which techniques are best suited for you and which aren't. After a while you will start putting it all together. You will begin to do things automatically.

In the martial arts, being like water helps one to develop a well-rounded game and to approach a problem with clarity and a fresh perspective. Think it. Act on it. And you too will see results, no matter what the endeavor.

THE OAK AND THE REEDS

In one of Aesop's fables titled The Oak and the Reeds a story is told of a mighty oak tree that was uprooted by a gale and fell across a stream into some reeds. "How have you reeds, so frail, survived, when I, so strong, have been felled?" asked the oak tree. "You were stubborn and wouldn't bend," replied the reeds, "whereas we yield and allow the gale to pass harmlessly by."

Remain open-minded and receptive to new ideas. Like the reeds you too will benefit from this approach.

CHINA HAS CONFUCIUS BUT
AMERICA HAS YOGI BERRA

Yogi Berra was a terrific baseball player, clutch hitter, and is now a Hall Of Famer. But as good as he was as an athlete, he will probably be most remembered for some of the statements he made to the press. Much of what he was quoted as saying may seem confusing until you think about it for a moment... then you discover a more profound meaning.

Here are a few of his quotes and my interpretations of the messages they convey.

If You Aren't Moving Forward You are Losing Ground

You had a great year. The best ever. This is not the time to get complacent. There are always areas for improvement. For example, making more personal calls, writing more letters, broadening your client base.

We Made Too Many Wrong Mistakes

Not getting the business or losing out to another company on a multi-year contract is certainly disappointing. Persevere. Do you think Jonas Salk discovered a polio vaccine on the first try? He certainly endured failure after failure before arriving at the cure. But his mistakes were right mistakes. Each taught him something that brought him closer to his goal.

A Nickel Ain't Worth a Dime Anymore
People are not logical about the way they perceive money and value. Rather than thinking about the price, think price presentations. Which is best, $18 per year or $1.50 per issue? How about $149.95 a month - or less than half a cent per minute? What do you think is perceived to be of greater value: an item that costs $1 each or 6 for $6? A little creativity will go a long way in helping to close a deal.

It Ain't Over Till It's Over
If there is one thing that's for sure in business, it is that nothing is for sure. Don't stop calling on those potentially lucrative accounts. Organizations restructure and people retire. Change is inevitable. New people have new ideas, a different way of doing things. When you are not getting the business, change gives you a reason to smile.

I'm So Busy But I Have So Much Time on My Hands
Never confuse activity with progress. Map out a strategy, do information gathering, plan ahead. Learn to identify the prospects and the suspects. Your time is finite. It is limited. Make good use of it and you will be handsomely rewarded.

It Was Hard To Have a Conversation With Anyone; There Were Too Many People Talking
In business as in personal life people underestimate the importance of listening.
Sometimes more can be gained by saying less. I remember a meeting I had with a prospective client. We did the normal salutations, then I asked a couple of probing questions. I maintained eye contact and nodded in agreement as he went into a discourse. He literally spelled out what I needed to do to get his business. I went back to the office, prepared a proposal, and a week later got the order. Folks, remember, this is selling not rocket science.

If You Can't Imitate Him, Don't Copy Him
If you are in a commodity business, you'd better do it faster and/or cheaper than the competition; otherwise, you are fighting an uphill battle.

Oxymorons may be based on contradictory thoughts but it was clear to me what Yogi was trying to say to all of you who make a living selling products and services.

YOU ARE WHAT YOU THINK

Our thoughts unquestionably affect our world and shape every aspect of our existence. The idea that we attract things to ourselves with our thoughts might seem controversial, but is there any doubt that people who have positive thoughts about their careers are more likely to attract promotions and raises than those who think of their work as an unpleasant chore? Or that people who have upbeat, positive attitudes about their fellow humans are more likely to attract friends than those who think everyone is against them?

Visualize your career and personal goals and replace negative thoughts about your problems with positive thoughts about the way you would like things to be.

It isn't our boss, our family, bad luck, or the economy that is holding us back – it's our own thoughts. The idea is to awaken and take control – choose what we want to be or have. It's up to us to make things right.

GUIDANCE IN AN OVERLOOKED PLACE

"Life is no straight and easy corridor along which we travel free and unhampered, but a maze of passages, through which we must seek our way, lost and confused, now and again checked in a blind alley. But always, if we have faith, a door will open for us, not perhaps one that we ourselves would ever have thought of, but one that will ultimately prove good to us."

A. J. Cronin
(Scottish novelist, dramatist, and
non-fiction writer)

CHAPTER V

THE X FACTOR

SETTLE FOR MORE

Excellence is doing ordinary things extraordinarily well. Excellence is the result of caring more than others think is wise, risking more than others think is safe, dreaming more than others think is practical, and expecting more than others think is possible.

THE HAVES AND
THE HAVE NOTS

Humanity is split into two classes of creatures:

The Haves - those who make great demands on themselves.

The Have Nots - those who demand nothing special of themselves.

Success is not predetermined at birth. The haves do what others won't, to achieve what others don't.

You are the person who has to decide whether you will do it or toss it aside. You are the person who makes up your mind whether you will lead or will linger behind. You are the person who will try for the goals that are or just be contented to stay where you are.

LAST MAN STANDING

In January, 2006, Ed Hearn began his quest to win the Toastmasters' International Speech Contest. No one thought he would win through a daunting gauntlet of 26,000 adversaries, many of them battle-tested over years.

As the months went by, Hearn's lark turned into a juggernaut. He won his club's contest, then area, division, district, and regional competitions as the initial 26,000 contestants were whittled down to ten for the finals held in Washington, D.C., in August.

Ed felt the chances of his winning the thing the first time out were slim and none. But the more he talked the more it seemed that his victory was a real possibility. He told of hours of practice, about taking on a speech coach later in the contest when he was beginning to look like a contender. He worked through hundreds of unsatisfying tweaks and four substantial re-writes of his speech. The speech was good, but Hearn wanted quintessential.

The title of his speech was "Bouncing Back," and the story he chose to tell was his own. He said he passed the Illinois bar exam only after taking it seven times. "They give it just twice a year, so during the time I was failing over and over, there were people who entered law school, graduated, and were practicing."

After his third try, Hearn decided the problem wasn't his knowledge but his approach to the test. He went over every question he missed in every test, looking for patterns.

After his sixth try, Hearn decided to stop seeking advice from successful people and seek out people who had multiple failures before rebounding. He said, "I'd ask them what they had done to turn things around."

He also worked on what he calls "exammanship" - becoming a better, more efficient test taker. "You can't be ignorant of the law," but there are ways to improve your chances. It took a while to figure them out, but now I could teach you how to pass in a week - maybe two."

Hearn comes across as likeable, self-deprecating, funny, and determined - ingredients in a whole stew of qualities that, together, seem winning to a lunch companion, a panel of twenty speech judges, or twelve jurors.

This story reminds me a lot of my years training in the martial arts. It is said that it takes three years to make a stance, three years to make a fist, and three years to make a punch.

Whether in life or in the martial arts, if one is to be proficient it takes commitment, patience, and preparation - all of the qualities that Ed Hearn displayed in an effort to be on the top of his game and the Last Man Standing.

CHANGING COURSE

Donald Rumsfeld, the former Secretary Of Defense, two days before he resigned, submitted a classified memo to the White House that acknowledged the Bush administration's strategy in Iraq was not working and called for a major course correction.

In my view it is time for a major adjustment, wrote Mr. Rumsfeld, who had been a symbol of a dogged stay-the-course policy. "Clearly, what U.S. forces are currently doing in Iraq is not working well enough or fast enough."

At the Pentagon, Mr. Rumsfeld had been famous for his "snowflakes" memos that drifted down to the bureaucracy from on high and that were used to ask questions, stimulate debate, and shape policy. Mr. Rumsfeld's memorandum circulated as
part of the administration's review of Iraq policy, was written in that spirit and with the same blunt aphorisms that Mr. Rumsfeld frequently used in public.

Most people find it difficult to admit to mistakes. The problem is that if you put off change for too long you compromise your ability to orchestrate it.

You make better decisions when you control the timing versus when acting out of desperation.

Mr. Rumsfield appeared to have put aside his ego and made an honest assessment of past efforts.

Though with change come risks, he, like all of us, took the first step toward making improvements.

Embracing change will give you the strength to endure instability and uncertainty - and the clarity to see positive results manifest themselves.

AVIDITY TO LEARN NEW THINGS

The sheer avidity to learn new things is one of the inherent traits of a successful salesperson. Without it you limit your ability to gain a competitive edge and to differentiate yourself from the rest of the pack.

Successful salespeople are not wedded to the status quo. They take calculated risks. They are innovators. They see the need to change as more desirable than the need to stay the same.

Try to learn something new every day and think how you might apply that information to winning new business and retaining customers.

Place a high value on curiosity and the avidity to know things and you too will begin to see positive results.

TEACHERS ARE STUDENTS TOO

We can gain wisdom and knowledge in the unlikeliest of places. From people who know more than we do and people who know less than we do. From people who mentor us to people who we teach and train.

In the martial arts we understand that students are teaching the teacher by being inquisitive, asking questions, and requiring us to find various ways for them to understand how to properly execute a technique when their athletic abilities, confidence levels, and temperament are different.

In our lives we often take one role or the other, positioning ourselves as either the expert or the untutored. But we should really be both. We should teach others and be willing to learn from them too. The teacher and the student are really one and the same.

EPILOGUE

I hope you have enjoyed this book and along the way realized some invaluable lessons.

You can choose to play the game of life with enthusiasm and vigor, displaying ethics and upholding your values, helping others to succeed, and being unafraid to fail.

You can choose to find new meaning and purpose in life or seize the opportunity to see your dreams come true.

You have the power to live life the way you choose, to be whatever you want to be, and find success where others have failed.

ABOUT THE AUTHOR

An entrepreneur and experienced corporate executive who oversaw a range of functions with emphasis on marketing, strategic planning, business development, and budgetary issues.

He is respected for his depth of knowledge, vision, and ability to see opportunities where others don't.

Darryl Reade is known for being adept at driving positive change, managing talent across a wide spectrum of disciplines, being a master at absorbing information, giving the data focus and meaning, and drawing the right conclusions.

He is a devoted family man and martial arts practitioner with a passion for helping others.